HOW I BUILT A 7 FIGURE LAW PRACTICE

WHILE SUFFERING FROM "LAW PTSD"

Learn what WORKS

&

What DOESN'T!

David Pisarra, Esq.

Printed in the United States of America

Published by:

American Ghost Media, LLC
1305 Pico Blvd
Santa Monica, CA 90405

Softcover ISBN:978-0-9994672-3-7

Ebook ISBN: 978-0-9994672-4-4

THE IDEAL PROFESSIONAL SPEAKER FOR YOUR NEXT EVENT!

Any law related organization or law firm that wants to develop their people to become better RainMakers needs to hire David Pisarra for a keynote and or workshop training.

TO CONTACT DAVID TO SPEAK:

David Pisarra, Esq.

310-664-9969

David@GlobalBusinessCoaching.com

TABLE OF CONTENTS

A NOTE ABOUT THE LAYOUT

I deliberately left a large margin on the outside edge at the request of a reviewer who wanted space to take notes. Knowing most lawyers like to annotate and highlight I thought it was a wise choice.

A THANK YOU GIFT

THANK YOU! I appreciate you buying this book and taking what little extra time you have to read it. As a Thank You Gift, you're entitled to a free month of unlimited email consultation with me.

Just send an email with subject BOOK THANK YOU to:

DAVID@GLOBALBUSINESSCOACHING.COM

INTRODUCTION

Woo Hoo!!!! I've won my Golden Ticket. That feeling of passing the bar is indescribable. I'm a modern day Charlie Bucket.

I can still remember the day I learned I passed. I swear the color of the sky was bluer, the trees were more picturesque and the air smelled sweeter. I smiled for a week.

Life changes when you're a member of the bar. As part of an elite cadre of people who are reputed to be rich, successful and happy by virtue of having a law degree and the right to practice in their chosen field people expect you to always have money and be content with your career.

But reality is different.

It's not so easy as the TV shows make it seem.

You have two paths laid out for you: Big Law - working for a firm with too many names on the letterhead. This path leads to 2,000 billable hours a year, a foreshortened life, and probably divorce (If you're lucky enough to find someone who will marry you knowing that you're never going to be around or worse, off the clock.) Your clients are forced upon you by senior lawyers, and it doesn't matter if you like or hate them, you have to represent them diligently. The big paycheck comes with a loss of autonomy. You may be lucky and have four weeks of vacation a year, but good luck being able to actually use it.

The second path is Be Your Own Boss - hang out a shingle and try to make it on your own.

I knew from the first day of law school that I was never going to be a Big Law kinda guy. I prefer to make my own hours, travel when I want, and be able to fire a client if they need to go from my life.

But that leads to the big question of having your own firm, "Are you really a lawyer without a client?"

So the first order of business is "GET A CLIENT!"

That's what this book is about. I've spent the last 20 years being the rainmaker in my firm. I'm the one who can walk into a room full of people I don't know, feel comfortable extending my hand and saying to people, "Hi, I'm David, what keeps you busy?"

Over the past two decades I've tried and succeeded and tried and failed at any number of publicity, marketing and advertising vehicles. I've made friends throughout Los Angeles and across the globe.

We've spent thousands of dollars on advertising, sometimes it works, sometimes it doesn't. I have war stories of public relations efforts and advertising fails.

I started out as a business development lawyer and my partner wanted to do family law. He thought, rightly, that it's an area of law that will never go away. My target clients were entrepreneurs who were clearly in need of legal advice and business savvy. I'd worked my way through law school doing small business turnarounds so I had seen upfront and personal most of the mistakes that new entrepreneurs make and was thinking that would be information people would pay for. I was wrong.

New entrepreneurs are leaving the corporate life for a reason - they want to be their own boss - they need to make their own mistakes and then pay lawyers ten times as much money to fix them as prevent them..

My job was to go out and find clients for our fledgling law practice so I'd find ways to meet people, start chatting them up, I'd share what I did, and mention what my partner did, and sure enough I'd leave with a client - for him. Family Law is a very popular practice and it is easy to find people who are in need of your services.

Before I knew it, my partner had a full calendar while I was still struggling to get clients for myself. Then it happened. One day he's double booked in court, and I have to cover for him. It was a pivotal point in our practice, in almost no time, my calendar was full with family law matters also, and the dream of being a business development lawyer was a fast fading memory in the rear view mirror of our practice.

Twenty years later and I'm suffering from extreme "Law PTSD". I'm literally throwing up pure bile one morning as I'm walking my dog at 5:00 a.m. out of anxiety, hurt and secondary trauma from my clients, who are mostly men at this point and essentially raw meat for the sausage factory of the Family Courts.

For at least the last five years I've been saying I need to get out of Family Law - "it's killing me." Finally in 2017 I take a baby step back into the world of business development, only this time it's working with a client as a coach. I'm mentoring him into a new business. We spend a weekend in a hotel conference room and come up with a business model and a strategy that he immediately begins to implement. Eighteen months later he calls me full of excitement and glee, 'Dave Dave Dave, we GOT THE CONTRACT!!!!"

I'm over the moon with joy for him. It feels so satisfying and rewarding to see the positive fruits of our collective efforts result in a new business being successful.

I want to do more of this business coaching, this mentoring people into work and careers they love. I have 20 years of trial and error in marketing, advertising, business management, client development, collateral design, video production, audio production and book publishing. I know I can use it for good and to help others who want to do more of the work they love.

This is for you, the lawyer who wants to reach more of your ideal clients, the lawyer who is on a mission to rebuild their brand and their practice. Here's my story of what has worked for me, and what hasn't, how things have changed over the years, and how it can benefit you.

Today I am a business coach who works with mid-career lawyers who are frustrated, burned-out and trying to find a way forward in their practice and their life. If that's you, there's a way to make your practice work if you want to reach more clients. If you're a mid-career lawyer who feels trapped in your practice due to family obligations, or partnership obligations, there's a way to a happier practice for you as well and together we can find it.

I hope that my 20 years of experience with all these ways to promote and market proves valuable to you, and I look forward to meeting you and hearing how you're succeeding in your life and practice.

Best Wishes,

David Pisarra, Esq.

NETWORKING

/'netwərkiNG/

noun

> *the action or process of interacting with others to exchange information and develop professional or social contacts.*

Either you love it, or you hate it, and I've found that most lawyers HATE it. For some reason lawyers seem to have an aversion to going out and pressing the flesh. I think it's because it all feels so "salesy" and "unprofessional" - as if letting people know what you're good at and how you can help them was a bad thing.

I get it though, salespeople have such a bad reputation and been the butt of so many jokes on tv that of course a member of the Bar who has spent years in college, and at law school doesn't want to be associated with the slimy and sleazy car salesman.

But that's not what I'm talking about. This isn't about trying to get your three best friends involved in an multi-level marketing scheme - this is about just letting people know that if they should ever be in trouble, you're there for them.

Now that's not so bad is it?

Chambers of commerce

Every new business owner thinks that they should join their local Chamber of Commerce as a way to immediate riches. Not so much.

The Chamber is more like a Slot Machine than a Gumball Machine. The reality is that we want the consistency of a gumball machine, the "insert a quarter, get out a piece of gum" but in reality it's much more like the slot machine, "insert a dollar, pull the handle, get nothing, insert a dollar, pull the handle get nothing, insert a dollar, pull the handle, win a dollar." Networking and marketing is not a one for one type of business. It's very frustrating because you can go for a year with just showing up at the cocktail reception, eat a few rumaki, and go home empty handed, or you can walk in, find a client immediately, and go another year before you ever land a second client.

What I've learned though is that if you go to serve, and have no agenda in mind of how many people you're going to meet, or how many clients you're going to land, but rather are there to contribute to the organization - you'll always get something back that is far more than you put in.

Volunteering

I was a member of the Business Alliance of Los Angeles in the early 2000's. At the time it was the premier gay and lesbian business association in the county. Subsequently it has merged with the West Hollywood Chamber of Commerce and is now the Los Angeles Gay and Lesbian Chamber of Commerce. I served for a few years on the board of BALA before I was elected President. As the President, a largely ceremonial position, my face and practice were promoted prominently to the membership and in the public relations outreach we did at the time.

To this day, a decade and a half later, I still have contacts from that period who send me clients, call on my expertise and refer me other clients. The amazing thing about being of service is the long legs that are developed and the relationships that help sustain me.

Being in a position of leadership was not only a great learning opportunity for me, but a wonderful way to gain positive exposure without having to "toot my own horn" - I let others do it for me. When I would be introduced the fact that I was a family lawyer was made known and I had the advantage of a third party doing the promotion for me.

Promotion Within The Chamber

It's my experience that working a Chamber can be great exposure and if you have the right leadership with the Chamber it's also a lot of fun.

On the other hand, with the wrong leadership, it can be a very negative experience. One of the things that I would do, is whenever I would attend an event I wrote up a quick one page recap and used that as a way to shine light on the other members. I would either print a hard copy and mail it out, or as times changed, I eventually would email it. There was one chamber leadership team that took great offense to my emailing the other members. They told me that I was "spamming them" and that I needed to cut it out. Now my attitude on this was that I was using the public email that was listed in the chamber directory and that since we were both chamber members, it was communication that would be at least welcome if not appreciated.

The leadership was having none of it. They were so offended by my promotional activity that they offered to return my dues and remove me from the membership.

On the opposite side of the spectrum was the West Los Angeles Chamber of Commerce who loved the idea of what I was doing so much they used to publicly thank me as they saw my emails as a way of keeping the membership engaged and active.

Sponsoring Events

Sponsoring events, taking a booth or an ad in a program is a very expensive way to get known in a community. It can be useful if you have something that makes you unique or is a natural for creating interaction with a crowd.

I've spent many an afternoon sitting in a 10x10 booth at a Chamber event. It involves having some well produced promotional items to hand out, and giving away a lot of free advice, in the hopes that one of these people will call on Monday and set an actual appointment. We've spent thousands of dollars on beautifully printed brochures, pens, footballs and other items that we are giving away. I've bought (and eaten) pounds of chocolate that was meant to increase our customer awareness.

After all these events, I'm not a big promoter of the idea that these are good for family law attorneys. The nature of what we do is so private and intimate, that the very public nature of a booth is offsetting. It likely works better for less intimate types of law like personal injury, worker's compensation, or estate planning.

Business Networking Groups

There are two very similar groups, the traditional Napoleon Hill style Mastermind Group and the more modern, sales focused "Networking Group". I cover the traditional groups in a separate section, later in this book.

I've been a member of several different business networking groups with varying degrees of success. BNI- Business Networking International, is a franchise model of bringing people together and is one of the most successful, when it works.

Each chapter is established and in theory as a member you are unique to your product or service for that chapter. That happens with varying degrees of purity. I've been to some chapters where there was only a single divorce lawyer, and others where there was the "divorce lawyer" and the "child custody lawyer" and the "child support lawyer" - the distinctions were minimal at best and designed to skirt the "rules" so that they could increase membership.

The various types of networking groups all have different rules and requirements. Some demand a certain level of attendance, others require a "referral" each week or a set number each month. Meeting formats vary also, from rigid with set times for the members to share their "elevator pitch" (that 10-30 second description of what makes you special) and speakers, to a very freeform agenda of getting to know each other. Being in a network one would think you could easily float from chapter to chapter - that's not always the case, it depends on the organization and their goals.

In Los Angeles, there is The Esquire Network which

is a better solution for many lawyers, as it is designed to expose you to other lawyers, their practices, and by extension their clients and even though you will have other lawyers in your area of practice that is a good thing, because even when we practice the same area, it doesn't mean we practice the same subspecialty. I focused on Father's and Parental Alienation, so when other family lawyers had cases that required that expertise, I was referred to, and then I would refer back to the Family Lawyer who worked in the Dependency Court, which is considered to be a sub-specialty of Family Law.

The fact of the matter is that you generally get out way more than you put in, so long as you put SOMETHING in. Even in groups where I have taken a very hands-off approach (not like me at all!) I have received business back.

Service Groups

Rotary

"Service above Self" is the motto of Rotary International and for almost 100 years that has served the members of RI well. They have done amazing good throughout the world, and their global efforts to eradicate polio have been largely successful. In 2018, there were only 29 cases reported worldwide, and that is largely due to the efforts of Rotary International.

I was a Rotary member for a few years, and I was

very active in my club. I attended weekly, I was frequently "touched" for "fines" which is Rotary-speak for fundraising. Basically if you have something noteworthy happen to you, the President will "fine" you a nominal amount, "David I see you're in the paper - AGAIN! I think that's worth a $5.00 fine." The money goes to a good cause so nobody really has an issue with it.

In terms of the networking, that's where Rotary shines but you also have to pick a good club and remember the Slot Machines vs Gumball Machine analogy. My particular club had about 100 members, most of whom were long time members - I mean decades worth - and frankly I was low man on the list of attorneys that were going to be referred to. That's okay, and I enjoyed my time there. I was the Editor of the newsletter for a year or so, and I made great friends out of Rotary.

It's an old school networking organization and I believe in its purpose and method, but I left when I became busy with other activities that were a higher priority. Two of the biggest benefits I received from Rotary were the connections to business leaders, and a dear friend who I still speak with regularly today.

Toastmasters

When someone wants to learn to become a better public speaker - Toastmasters is the Gold Standard for that education. I joined Toastmasters International in 2010. My club, Westside Toastmasters, is a robust club with over 40 regular members, from probably 15 different countries.

I joined because I wanted to practice my public speaking and frankly the judges don't give good feedback on your performance and what you can do to be more entertaining and effective. Jumping in with both feet I found that the process of learning how to be a better speaker was both enjoyable and easy. The TI manual at the time was a 10 speech workbook that stepped you through the elements of effective communication.

When I first started I think our dues were $75 for 6 months, and today it's increased all the way to a huge $105 for 6 months. Because of the friends I've made and the work that has been referred to me through my club I think I can pay my dues for the rest of my life and I'll still be ahead of the game.

The beauty of being a Toastmaster is that I can travel the world and attend other clubs and make friends. So in a city like Los Angeles where we have over 100 clubs I have a far reaching community within an hour or two's drive. When I travel the world I have had the joy of attending other clubs, like the Ajijic Toastmasters in Ajijic Mexico, which is a dual language club, and they alternate between English and Spanish.

But TM is not just a speaking program. I's also a leadership program that helps people learn leadership skills as they run the clubs. There is an entire training program on leadership that is included in the monthly dues.

Overall I highly recommend being involved in Toastmasters International if you need to polish your speaking skills, want to develop those leadership skills or just expand your referral pool and meet interesting people.

Board Members

As a lawyer the opportunities for you be of service to non-profits is literally endless. You are viewed as both a financial resource for your own cash donations, a resource for the other rich people you know (clients and other lawyers) and resource for free legal advice and service on the board.

Be careful what non-profits you become involved with as they will gladly take all your time, coyly look to you for lots of donations, and may or may not have the connections you need to make it all worthwhile.

On the one hand, it can be a tremendous door opener when you are in a well established, well connected non-profit that has a large board and/or donor base that will be needing your services at some point. On the other hand, a newly established non-profit that does not have a robust board may not be the best use of your networking time.

The lack of a robust board can also be an indicator of organizational rot. Poor leadership will usually have a hard time keeping a good board, and you should be on the lookout for that. Indicia of bad leadership is heavy rotation of staff and board members - that means the time you spend developing good relationships could all be wasted if the non-profit or individual board members lose interest.

My experience with one board was that they had a great non-profit topic (youth) and they had connections to the entertainment industry, but the leader had his own ego so inflated that it overshadowed the good that was done. His own inability to lead a good board meeting led to a high turnover in the board, and eventually I left after my term was up. I have little tolerance for poorly run meetings. I expect them to run on time, and not get bogged down in minutiae. We're the board we set policy, raise money and throw events that are either fundraisers or friend raisers. When I was spending two hours of my precious life in petty details that are better left to staff, I knew it was time to leave.

I highly recommend that if you are going to be involved with non-profits that you have clear boundaries on your time and commitments. Spend more than you think necessary in vetting a non-profit - it's not just a quick Charity Navigator and Megan's List review to decide if you should be involved. Speak with the current (and past if you can find them!) board members and see if they are getting out of the experience what you hope to get.

Public Speaking

If you enjoy public speaking like I do, the benefits to your practice can be immense. I have several speeches that I make available to non-profits, social service clubs and anyone that will listen to me. I have spoken on domestic violence, divorce planning, substance abuse, and podcasting for professionals. I have spoken to Rotary clubs with 5 members and I've travelled to New Zealand to speak to a room full of professional speakers about how to use a podcast to promote themselves.

Rotary/Elks/Moose/Eagles/Water Buffalo

I wrote about being part of a Rotary Club as a member, but there's another way in that will allow you to reach their members, but not as regularly and that is offering to speak to their club. Most social service clubs meet either weekly or bi-weekly and have some sort of speaker each week. For the president or whomever is doing the scheduling that is a a heavy burden to carry, and if you can contact them and offer to do a speech your chances of being booked are almost certain. I've never been turned down by a chapter for a speaking opportunity - I may have been put on the calendar months out, but they always take me.

Toastmasters

Once you're a member of Toastmasters International, it is very easy to get on a neighboring club's agenda with a speech. If you approach the President and ask to be able to come present they will almost always say yes. Don't go in with a blatantly obvious sales pitch. Have a subtle message that is woven into your speech that communicates what it is you do and you'll be invited back anytime.

Personally I used my speech on the subject of male victims of domestic violence as a way to reach other clubs and promote myself as a family law attorney but did so in a manner that I was educating the audience and bringing them value. You can do the same with your area of expertise.

Places of Worship

If you are a regular member of a house of worship odds are that you could be do a free seminar that is informative to the other members and have the weekly/ monthly newsletter do a write up on it before or after so that you reach all the membership.

When you are "helping" the community it will reflect back on you in positive ways. This will make you the go-to person in that area.

Los Angeles Domestic Violence Council

Depending on your area of practice there is likely some governmental body that has legislative concerns you can become involved with as a way to promote yourself. For me it is the Los Angeles Domestic Violence Council.

I've been attending their meetings for a few years now, and was recently asked to participate in a panel discussion. Being on that dais with other luminaries and experts puts me in their same category which only helps raise my profile and my perceived celebrity.

Bar Associations & Big Firms- MCLE's

You're an expert in something. Odds are that there's a way to take that expertise and turn it into an MCLE that you can use to either speak to other lawyers at bar association meetings, or you can do what I did and market my MCLE to big law firms that need to have the hours for their partners. I was brought in to do a "Lunch and Learn" for several big firms and it was a great way to get exposure for my firm

Substance Abuse

I present an MCLE on Substance Abuse, which in California is a mandatory class for all attorneys, and a hard one for most association and firms to get live. By having a specialty course I make myself more attractive to a wider group of attorneys (effectively all of them) rather than just those who might want to learn about the intricacies of Family Law.

Domestic Violence

I teach an MCLE on Domestic Violence, which in California is NOT a mandatory class for all attorneys (YET!), but it is one that affects many areas of law these days and is becoming a more requested topic. As the subject matter is more interesting to people than a boring class on division of 401(k)s it usually pulls pretty well in terms of interest and I have enough wild stories to make the hour go pretty quickly.

The question for you is what type of interesting subject matter can you speak on for 50 minutes that is of general interest that will let people know your specialty and what type of clients you are looking for?

Breakfast Seminar for Therapists

I have no idea how many bagels I have bought for therapists over the years, but I know that they have resulted in many referrals to my office. Finding and nurturing a supporting trade/profession is a big key to success in this world. I have sent most of my clients to therapists, and occasionally some of them even go.

This doesn't have to be a major expense, if you can find a local coffee shop/ diner that has a back room they may let you have the room for a low or free fee, in exchange for a minimum food buy. Alternatively you may find that with a room rental fee, you don't have to buy food, the guests then can order a la carte, and you can then invite as many participants as the room will hold.

Making the list of who to invite was a simple matter of going down the phone list from the yellow pages (in the olden days) these days it's a simple Google search and a cut and paste into a database. I'd use the Call Send Call method of outreach. You Call and leave a message (since you're most likely going to be sent to a voicemail - especially with therapists/psychologists) the message is simple "Hi this is David Pisarra, a family law attorney in town and I'm hosting a breakfast for therapists and would like to invite you to this free event next Tuesday at 7:00 a.m. I'll send an email with the particulars. Have a great day!"

I'd follow up with an email and then the next day I'd call to confirm receipt of the email and hopefully get them on the phone to chat.

The whole process is very easy, user friendly and doesn't have that Cold Call feel to it where I'm trying to sell them something.

Law Day for 'Handel OnTheLaw'

Bill Handel has built a radio career out of his call-in show telling people "how they don't have a case." It's his tagline and it's worked very well for him over the past 20 plus years. His show is syndicated and he's found ways to monetize it beyond just the regular adverts on the air. He has an annual "Law Day with Handel on the Law" where law firms spend various amounts of money on promotional items that they bring this event. Some of the slots are paid for, but I've gone in the past and not had to pay for a table.

The basic idea is that the public is going to come and speak to an attorney about their individual problems and you as the lawyer will hopefully land a new client or two.

Some areas of the law are very popular, this past year the guy across from me at the tax table was very popular- I was more like an afterthought of someone who came there to talk about their Lemon Law car.

But other years it's been a very rewarding experience. Like most of the efforts in the marketing and advertising space - it's all slot machines not gumballs.

Some law firms spend a great deal of money on flags, banners, table top displays, videos on repeat loops, pens, squeezes balls, brochures, bottle openers. Others just show up with a lawyer and a pad of paper. I'm not sure which is more effective. It's important to be comfortable and be you.

ADVERTISING

"I know I'm wasting half my advertising dollars—I just don't know which half."

This famous saying has been attributed to David Ogilvy, the grandfather of modern advertising, and many others who want to claim credit for it. Who actually said it is not the important part. The thought behind it is what matters. It's a hard truth and you have to just accept that about half the hard earned money you spend on advertising will be wasted. That's why you have to have a high ticket item to sell. Luckily for us, as lawyers, our fees generally are high enough that we can absorb the costs, even though they are frustrating and annoying to pay.

Over the years I've tried just about every advertising vehicle I could find in an effort to reach some sort of stable flow of clients, and I've yet to do it.

The harsh reality is that the life of an entrepreneur lawyer is a rollercoaster ride and you have to be able to juggle several different hats simultaneously - or decide to outsource your marketing management. It's time consuming to attend bar association meetings, find, pitch and speak at a Rotary club, and remember that you have deadlines for your advertising copy to be submitted. Shooting videos and recording podcast episodes all while finding time to post compelling content on your Facebook wall, shoot an amazing picture for Instagram, write the copy, add in the 11- 30 hashtags that apply to that picture and write a blog post that you can crosspost over to LinkedIN. And on top of all that, you STILL have to practice LAW!

So we try everything to make it easier to find clients. Here are some of the ways that I have, some of them have worked well, others not so much:

Val-Pak

Yes, that monthly mailer that has 3 different car washes, a dry cleaner and the town's dentist along with two pizza parlors is a place to advertise. I know you think it's "beneath me" as a lawyer to advertise in such a lowbrow medium, but let me tell you, I spent a few hundred dollars and was retained by a client for a civil suit / business partnership dispute. I was advertising estate planning. You never know what you'll end up with in the wacky world of advertising.

A properly constructed ad, one that is eye-catching, and markets your services well, can succeed in the direct mail world of Val-Pak. I would recommend practice areas like Estate Planning, which is going to appeal to retired people who are more likely to open the Val-Pak. I'd also look at services that are focused on stay at home parents, like Divorce and Child Custody matters.

Newspapers

Newspapers have two types of advertising for sale: Display and Classified. Classified is for garage sales, selling a used car, finding a nanny. Do NOT waste your money on classified - no matter what the salesperson tells you about how effective they are. THEY ARE NOT GOOD FOR LAWYERS.

Display Advertising is for products or services from companies. It's sold in column inches usually or as a fraction of a page (1/4, 1/2, 1/3, etc) Display ads are what everybody thinks of when they say advertising in print.

A good display ad can be a great way to raise overall awareness that you exist as a service provider. Remember most people are not looking to hire you at this particular moment. That means that any display ad campaign needs to be exactly that - A LONG RUNNING CAMPAIGN. This is the biggest of the Slot Machines.

You may hit it big with an ad in the paper, but don't expect it to happen any time soon.

You have two main costs with Display Ads - the actual ad space, and the design cost. Most publications will gladly have an in-house person do the design work for you - but they will usually not be super creative or come up with a unique design for you. They'll generally just recycle some older, previously used style and just swap out the particulars of your contact information. This is not a bad thing, but it's not a great thing either.

If you want to have unique artwork, you need to hire your own designer. They can be found inexpensively on Fiverr, gigaom, gig salad, Craigslist, NextDoor and at any community college. Of course you can spend thousands on a designer at a high end design firm - generally not necessary unless you're planning on full-on media campaign and then you probably have a Public Relations (PR) firm working for you.

Yellow Pages

In the dark ages, we used to have these things called phone books. They were three inches thick and listed everyone's home address and their phone number. The commercial part of the book would be printed on yellow paper, hence the name. Lawyers would take out full page ads, with splashy four color printing and special 800 phone numbers to track the responses. These would costs tens of thousands of dollars. We spent $25,000 for a full page ad and I think we received 2 phone calls, one from a potential client that couldn't afford us, and a second from a salesman for another phone book....

Today the phone book is a distant memory, but there are still online services that use listings to act in a similar fashion and I suggest that you take advantage of them. Frequently they have differing levels of service available to you as an advertiser. The free level is usually the basics of a listing - the bare minimums, but you can add in a website link, a map, a video, photos of offices etc for an additional monthly or annual fee.

My firm is listed with YP.com, HG.com and the GayellowPages.com. I don't pay for premium listings with them, but they are available, and expensive, and I'm doubtful that the additional cost would give me a good Return on Investment, based on the calls I receive now from them. However, the backlinks and the SEO value of being listed here is helpful.

Radio Spots

The Radio can be a great resource for advertising if you service the audience well. For example, on sports radio stations Criminal Defense (DUI especially) does very well, Bankruptcy, Tax and Worker's Compensation all reach the needs of that audience. We tried Family Law and were not happy with the results. Our ad used the on-air talent to speak so that we have the credibility of their celebrity to increase the response rate. Didn't work well for us.

Sports Bar Menus

As our practice is focused on the needs of fathers and husbands, I figured that an ad in a menu at a sports bar would do well. I was completely wrong. I have no idea why. We spent a few thousand dollars to have thousands of menus printed and distributed to Hooters across the Los Angeles basin and not one time did we get a phone call from it.

Live and learn.

Bus Benches

I've always wanted to do bus bench advertising as I figure it's seen by a lot of cars, people who are driving around all day and would be able to get the information on how to contact us. My partner has always vetoed it. It's one of two things he's vetoed in my 20 years trying things, so I can't complain, he's certainly allowed me to try some wacky things!

But I notice that there are a lot of attorneys advertising on bus benches for Worker's Compensation, Lemon Law, Personal Injury, Social Security Disability, Traffic Ticket disputes, and Bankruptcy. Stands to reason that a Family Law ad could do well, and Estate Planning as well.

I think that an ad that is pretty clear on its purpose, and with a large phone number could do well. You don't have to put your face on every ad, and even your firm name can be in small print if you're squeamish about being known as the 'bus bench lawyer.'

Buses

Continuing with the theme here, the buses themselves can now be wrapped in full color vinyl ads as well as the side panels and the overhead inside panels. It seems to me that if your clients are normally riding the bus anyways, why not advertise where they are? This would likely be for the Worker's Compensation, Bankruptcy, and Labor Law practices.

Again, I've not been allowed to try this, but given the number of ads that I see as fully vinyl wraps for personal injury lawyers, it seems to me that they must be working.

Sky-Writing and Sky Banners

Got your attention didn't I?   You thought - no way!

You're right.

I just had to put this in here for the fun of it. No I haven't tried it, and I haven't even seen other lawyers try it, and it seems to me that this would generally be a waste of time and money, unless you paired it with some sort of stunt or other way to maximize the impact. If you were a firm that specializes in aviation law and/or insurance, then sponsoring an air show and having a sky-writer may work as a fun stunt. I would suggest having it videotaped so that you could use it in both television and print ads.

ONLINE SERVICES

LegalMatch.com

This is a subscription model of finding clients. The main website has potential clients post a description of their needs and then an announcement is sent out to the attorneys who have subscribed to that topic area.

I've used LegalMatch.com at varying times and what I've found is that if I respond VERY quickly, and more importantly, with a customized message to the poster, then I have a good chance of at least speaking to the client.

Many lawyers use just a reformatted response to a request for information and I know that I beat them in the race to create client connection - because that's what my clients tell me.

We're in a relationship business, and unless you're doing a type of law that is commoditized, (and then you're competing on price!) you have to make an connection with the client so they feel comfortable entrusting you.

When I was doing research on LegalMatch.com to decide if I wanted to sign up and pay them a hefty monthly fee, (it approaches a thousand dollars a month) I created a bogus client profile to see what my competition was doing. I made it an enticing enough divorce and custody case that I figured every lawyer in the area of practice and geographically close to me would jump on it.

I received six responses. All six were boring pre-formatted statements about how wonderful the lawyer was and why I should be honored to have them represent me. None of them addressed the issues in my profile, none of them referenced my particulars and none of them were persuasive. They were like little lego pieces - totally interchangeable.

They didn't stand out at all.

I was not able to differentiate any of them based on the responses, which means that if they are all alike, I'm going to pick the one who is cheapest. That's no way to run a law practice - competing on price is race to the bottom for all of us.

When I created a law practice that was marketed to men, I was told "you're losing half your market!" Maybe. But my experience was that I had an easier time standing out and being recognized. The clients that were my ideal clients found me much more readily. I had a clear message resonated with them and I spent much less time trying to convince them to hire me, because they came in already wanting to hire "The father's rights guy". Plus, I still cultivated a good number of female clients who wanted what we offered, because they were the "man in the relationship" and the primary provider who had the stay at home partner.

Thinking that you are going to lose clients by going narrow and deep is a fallacy. You gain influence, speed of recognition and it will be easier to target your ideal client.

AVVO.com

This is a legal focused website that lists and rates attorneys. Every attorney is listed, but only a few of them take the time to properly build out their profiles. I did mine years ago, had some fellow attorneys and prior clients go on and give me a review so that my overall profile rating is improved. There is a community forum to add in articles and answer questions from the public. I've submitted a few articles and answered a few questions so that I have a robust presence.

Of course there is an upgraded profile option for a fee and loads of advertising options. You can pay for a display ad that will present you and your subject areas in a separate box when someone does a search. There is Premium Listing in both topic areas and geographic locations so that you can drill down into specifically what and where you want to be known. For example we have an exclusive on Uncontested Divorces in the

Westside of Los Angeles and the South Bay. Ads are sold in blocks of 100 ads served up each month, and you can control your budget by choosing how many blocks you want to purchase.

In highly profitable and competitive areas of the law like Criminal Defense and Divorce the blocks are pricey but in other areas they become more affordable but also less profitable. It's just a matter of spending what you want to earn what you want.

YELP.com

The review site that started out for restaurants and quickly has become a major force in the world of review sites for all sorts of different products, services and businesses. They have changed their business model from what used to be a straight up flat fee each month, to a more budget conscious per search/ad served model. Like AVVO, there is a premium listing ability, and you can upload pictures and videos and build out a profile that lists opening hours, map locations and descriptions of services and "Specials" (for example, if you want to offer a $100 off your legal bill or maybe a Free Consultation.)

The public has the right to review you and you develop a Star Rating based on the cumulative reviews. In the world of lawyers, odds are that you will get a bad review or two. As the "owner" you have the option to respond with your side of the story. Having a negative review removed is nigh on impossible, however as you develop more positive reviews the negative ones seem to fade into the background. Also YELP claims they don't give preference for paying advertisers versus non-paying businesses, but it does seem like negative reviews are more prominent on unpaid business reviews...

Yodle.com

Here's another web-based service that promised us tremendous results and it didn't bear out. Yodle uses a separate tracking phone number and a website to geolocate leads and phone calls for our services. They were moderately expensive - in the mid hundreds - and it has great reporting capabilities, but in the end we didn't generate enough actual business to justify the costs.

SEO Wizards

I'm sure you've received an email a week, if not a day, about how "SEO wizards" guarantee you first page on Google, or some such thing. For a low monthly fee they will put you on the first page. I've done my research on this, and this is generally a bad idea.

Companies that promise you a particular result are probably using what is called "Black Hat" practices. They can get you there, for a short period of time, based on some unethical and unrepeatable tricks of the trade. Once the big search engines find out you're doing it, you face the prospect of being downgraded and/or blacklisted which means your efforts are not only backfiring, but going to cost you a lot more money in the future to fix, if you even can.

Bottom line: if it sounds too good to be true….

GoogleAds

Ah the big daddy of advertising these days. Truth is, Google can make you a ton of money - and they're going to get their share.

GoogleAds are where it's at for most attorneys advertising these days - or so it seems. The competition for good keywords - those high value search terms that people are using - is fierce. You can spend a huge amount of money fighting to get noticed in a sea of lawyers who all want to throw money at a problem, and many have the funds to make the fight expensive.

If attorney rates are a race to the bottom in some ways, the race to advertising domination is an arms race that can bankrupt you. There literally is no limit to the amount of money you can spend in GoogleAds because it's an auction for eyeballs.

The answer then is two-fold: 1) pick a few search terms that best describe what your real and ideal clients are searching for and use those to build a GoogleAd Campaign around, 2) Set a budget and know that it's a slot machine gamble each month, and over the long term arc of a year, it will probably pay for itself if you have targeted adequately.

The promise of "turning the tap on new clients" is a great idea, but not always true. You have to remember that most clients are not looking to hire an attorney in the next 10 seconds, which is about as long as they will be looking at your website. It's about awareness building. This is where the remarketing process can be useful.

Remarketing is the process where once a potential client has visited a site, it shows back up in their other searches. It's the way that you go to visit Dick's Sporting Goods looking for hip waders and for the next two weeks all you see are outdoors ads...

BingAds

BingAds are the little stepsister to GoogleAds - they're the Microsoft version of the behemoth that is Google. I've used them and they are just as effective, and expensive and I've notice no discernible difference in the quality of the clients or phone calls I received from potential clients - just that they were less likely to be Apple users.

TRADITIONAL MEDIA

I'm a media whore.

I embraced that fact years ago, and frankly any attorney who wants to build a practice or be the firm's rainmaker should expect to be the same, called the same, and embrace the mantle. Besides - it's pretty fun!

Traditional media is the newspaper, television and radio shows that we grew up with. The many reports of its demise are false. It's changed certainly, and the market is not nearly as narrow as it was in the days of three television stations and only AM radio.

Newspapers are still produced, though the death of the afternoon edition is true. But the rise of the longer form weekly, and the hyper local model of publishing has grown, so it's all a tradeoff.

I loved being on television, and no I wasn't the guy running ads, I was seen on a roundtable show positioned as a legal expert. That's valuable in the long run, and cheaper than putting up ads three times an hour.

Week in Review

Cable companies have a legal obligation to provide community access videos. They're not nearly as common these days as the industry has consolidated and the lobbyists have done their job in Washington, but they still exist. In the early 2000s there was a show in Los Angeles called Week in Review and it was a political roundtable show, with four guest contributors, a host, and three rotating guests. I was one of the semi-regular contributors and my "slot" was the liberal democrat gay male voice who was also a lawyer.

The reach of this show was literally all across the state of California as Adelphia Cable would distribute the show to their sister companies for wider exposure. It helped that the original host was the President of Adelphia Bill Rosendahl, who went on to become a Los Angeles City Councilmember.

I talked my way on to the show originally by sending a couple of pitches to the producer and being willing to jump on stage on 15 minutes notice.I made myself available to her, and to keep the show interesting she wanted to rotate the contributors. Once I was in the rotation it was fairly easy to become more regular by being a good guest, one that contributed some spice, allowed the other guests to speak and occasionally got a bit heated, but not so much as to be offensive.

Being on that show was a blast, and I wish they still had it today. I was not only recognized often from that show, but I had many clients come to me from it. Even though I may have been on speaking about public policy towards homelessness, I was seen as an expert in family law because the chyron, that lower third of the screen had my name and the description I asked for. So people were seeing me on their televisions with the Adelphia logo, and "David Pisarra, Family Law Expert / Father's Rights" and the credibility of the corporation carried to me.

That's how celebrity works, you can leverage others fame into boosting your own. There's a certain family that has done that quite well.....

Santa Monica Daily Press Column

In my first year of practice I rented an office and one afternoon there's a knock on the door from a advertising sales guy. "HI! We're starting a newspaper in town and would you like to advertise?"

"Hi, not really. But I'd love to write for you."

"Oh I can't help you with that, you'll have to speak to the Editor."

So I wrote the Editor saying I wanted to write for her paper. I thought a Legal Views and News column would be good community service and that the exposure would help my office.

She sent back a request for a sample column.

I sent her two columns, and a list of 52 topics, one for each week of the year to show that I had ideas and content and was dedicated to writing.

"You start Tuesday" was what I got back.

18 years later, and four Editor changes, and I'm still writing for them on a weekly basis. Over the years I've received dozens of clients who come to me because they see me in the paper weekly. My column takes anywhere from 1-3 hours week to write, depending on the topic.

Is it worth it? Absolutely. I'm seen as an expert, a local celebrity and it's a great way for me to engage in the writing process that I love. Over the years I've improved in my speed of writing, the quality of my work has improved (so I'm told!) and I've now written over 1,000,000 words, which is an accomplishment in itself.

Radio Shows

Guesting on a radio is not as hard to do as you may think. There are over 10,000 shows that need 4,000 guests - daily. That's a lot of opportunities if you do a minimal amount of effort to reach out and become known as an expert in your field.

For me, I would send out press releases to various producers on topics that were of interest that day or week. Having a Valentine's message from a divorce lawyer was a fun way to lighten up a show. Using the latest big Hollywood breakup as a foothold also works well. Brad and Angelina helped many an attorney make their mortgage payments....

I recommend picking one or two shows the are a good

fit in both their audience, and your target clients, and the show hosts style. It may take a few attempts to be noticed, but once you are on their radar you should be called.

Once you're there, now you can use the logos from the station on your website and that will help build your credibility as a 'known celebrity' for potential clients, and also for other media that are doing background research.

I've been contacted by the BBC who found my website and then wanted me to opine on some case. It's pretty cool when it starts to build on itself and they start calling you!

LEGAL MEDIA

How many legal journals and magazines do you receive each month? I get about 6 and I'm not even paying for them! That means there is a lot of content that must be created each month.

All of those journals are looking for new angles, new stories, anything that will engage their readers and make them open up the magazine again next month. What that means for us is with a bit of creativity and some moxie, we can get in those journals and magazines as contributing writers.

One of the books I wrote is called ***What About Wally? Co-parenting a Pet with an Ex***. It's the story of how my former boyfriend and I continue to parent our dog. The first half of the book is a memoir and the second half is a Parenting Plan that was taken from one of my child custody cases and reworked.

That's a unique story, and one that landed me on the back page of California Lawyer Magazine. All I had to do was send a pitch letter to the Editor that took about 4 minutes to write. It can be done in this easy to use format:

TO: EDITOR@CALLAWYER.COM

SUBJECT: Story Pitch: _____

Hi,

Would the story below work for you?

David Pisarra, Esq.

_____

HOW TO SHARE A DOG AFTER A BREAKUP

Divorce Attorney Shares Pet Parenting Plan

When Family Law Attorney David Pisarra and his boyfriend split up, the relationship ended, but the responsibility for Dudley the dachshund continued. This is their story of how to share a pet, and learn to be friends after a relationship......

It really is that easy. You want to have a clear pitch to the Editor, who has a few SECONDS to read your Subject Line, the Headline and the Sub-head and will decide if they're going to continue. So you need to make it snappy and clear.

LOCAL BAR ASSOCIATIONS

Local bar associations often have their own magazines or newsletters and they need content as well. The San Fernando Valley Bar association put out a call for papers and a friend of mine wanted to write a piece and asked me to co-author. We wrote a piece on Domestic Violence and Family Law and both of us were listed as authors.

The divorce industry is rife with publications, and one of them is Family Law Magazine. They wanted an article on Pet Law. Well guess who has a book on that, and it was an easy sell to become the writer so I could get my name and website listed.

Traditional media is not dead, it's just changed. The opportunities are out there for all of us, if we just do a bit of legwork, and get over the hebby-jeebies of self-promotion.

DIGITAL MEDIA

Oh the exciting world of digital media! It means that you can share your thoughts, emotions and feelings with the entire world at the click of a button.

How cool is that? And scary. And overwhelming. And anxiety inducing, it brings up all our most basic fears - "I don't want the whole world to hear/see me? What if I'm bad on camera? Or worse, say something stupid?"

Here's the good news, yes the whole world COULD see/hear you. Here's the better news, MOST OF THEM WONT EVER KNOW ABOUT YOU.

Seriously. There's about 7.5 BILLION people on the planet. They are not looking for you.

Only a tiny number of people reach the status of the most well known people on the planet - the Oprahs, the Barack Obamas and the Queen of England. Global names are few and far between. For example, do you know who Michael Schumacher is?

No. You don't. Unless you happen to be a Formula One fan, preferably from Europe, male, and in the 30-60 age range. He is a HUGE celebrity on the car racing circuit. One of the most recognizable faces ever - to his fans.

If he was sitting next to you at a restaurant, odds are you'd have zero idea who he was.

That's celebrity for you. It's great in a vertical, but outside of that community, you'll probably not be recognized.

Building a community around you of people who love your subject, love what you say, and want to get to know, like, and trust you is simultaneously easy in that digital media makes it a simple process these days, and difficult in that rising above the cacophony of other voices is not so simple.

Put your fears away. You will not be swamped with rabid autograph hunters who make your life a living hell. Unless you want them to, I promise.

Be bolder and more vocal in what you do, who you serve and get your name out there. Here's how I do it:

Men's Family Law Podcast

About five years ago I was at breakfast with my friend Mark and he looks up at me, says, "You talk a lot. Some of it is even good. You should have a podcast."

"Thanks, sounds good. What's a podcast?"

"Go listen to Joe Rogan, and Dave Ramsay"

So I did, and then a bunch of other shows and realized that this new medium of audio was basically an on-demand radio show that would allow me to become a celebrity, an educator, and to answer those same 10 questions that everyone asks me about family law.

The Men's Family Law podcast was launched and today stands at 50 episodes of content that is evergreen - meaning it's not tied to the news cycle. That means I can recycle postings and continue to have it available as a marketing tool to keep my name top of mind for people.

I've used my podcast to interview an NBA owner, a psychotherapist, a major journalist and a dating coach, I've spoken with Mark "SealFIT" Divine, and Diamond Dallas Page through my show. It's an amazing tool to open doors and create increased celebrity for me, which makes the client conversion process go much quicker and easier. By the time they have listened to a few of my shows, heard how I interact with people, and maybe bought my book off the website, they're already sold on me, and it's just a matter of them sending me a retainer.

Podcast Hosting and Guesting

For you there are two paths to podcasting glory: 1) create your own show - it's much easier than you think. Literally you can record episodes on your phone and upload them the internet for a very basic solution, and 2) you can start by being a guest on shows. As a podcast host, I can say that I rarely receive guest requests, but when I do they are not only welcomed, but when the guest is a good fit, I appreciate the fact that I don't have to track them down. The less work you make a host do, the more likely it is for your request to result in a YES. Send them a request that includes what you want to talk about, why you want to talk about it, how it will help their audience, and include an introduction/bio for yourself and you're now ahead of 90% of the people who ask for appearances.

YouTube Channel

I have videos up on my MensFamilyLaw YouTube channel that are designed to be 3-5 minute short explanations of the most commonly asked questions. They're not great videos. In some of them I look TERRIBLE. But the content is good and for someone who is looking for answers what they care about is the information, not the video.

The return on my investment has been tremendous. I bought a $400 camera, I already had a MacBook to do my video editing on, and the YouTube account is free. The first videos I did took a bit of time to edit in iMovie, but surprisingly it is much easier than you think to edit a movie where you are just standing against a wall and talking. (Francis Ford Coppola I'm not!)

They're great because I can use them on my Facebook on my AVVO profile, and on my website.

Today, it's even easier to make a video as the smartphone has taken over the planet. You can literally record a video, upload from your phone, and you're online. Think about every time you answer a call from a potential client. Once you hang up, just hit the record button and share the advice you just gave away for free. Obviously people are needing it, and you're going to do it anyways, so why not do it once and use it as marketing for the rest of your life? That way when the next call comes in, the potential client is pre-sold on you as their attorney.

How can you not want to do this? It takes 5 minutes and you live on the web forever....

HollywoodLife.com

Thank God for Hollywood and it's endless need for gossip and updates about what the stars are doing today! I've been a resource for exclusive content to hollywoodlife.com for a couple of years now. The Brad and Angelina divorce and custody battle led to many many articles and conversations between me and a host of reporters.

The key to my success with reporters is that I am always available to them and give them my mobile number, I always take their call, or I call them back immediately. Being in the news industry, time is critical, they have deadlines and if you can't help them, they'll move on to the next lawyer.

GoodMenProject.com

The GoodMenProject.com is an online magazine style

website devoted to male issues and having "the conversation that no one else is having." I found it to be a great place to promote myself and my writing because I could tackle topics the were too hot for other websites. I wrote about contraception, male survivors of abuse, and domestic violence among other topics. The audience is mostly male they get it, and they would refer me business. Plus the biggest value is the backlinks (the posting of my website url on the GoodMenProject site) that I received to my main website which were listed in my biography and in my articles.

This is where I learned that the whole world is not looking for you. I could write things that were more specific for my audience and realized after awhile that my other clients weren't reading them.

If you need to establish yourself as an authority, finding a website and audience like GoodMenProject and becoming a contributor is great way to expand your exposure.

Divorce360.com

Here's the other end of the spectrum, Divorce360 was a website that was devoted to all things divorce but with a primarily female audience. No great surprises there in terms of audience; most of the time the woman is researching years in advance of the actual filing. So what was I doing there? I wrote pieces that were child custody focused, advocating for a 50/50 custodial time share. Did I get the exposure I wanted? Yes, but I also got the backlinks, and those were more powerful for me, because they raised my ranking in the Google algorithm of site ranking. That meant that I wasn't paying to appear on first page, I was just appearing organically, which has much greater value.

SOCIAL MEDIA

Social Media is touted as the greatest thing to hit humanity since the printing press. I'm not sure I agree, especially since as a divorce lawyer I've seen so many marriages finally succumb to the courts with the allure of that long lost high school sweetheart, who is also going through a breakup...

In today's environment we have so many ways to connect with each other, and even people we don't know and will likely never meet, that the attraction to spending too much time online is actually becoming a psychological disorder.

Personally I've spent way too much time on sites like Facebook, Twitter and Instagram. Who hasn't fallen into a cheesy pizza video hole and lost 20 minutes of their life?

But the question for us is, can you make good marketing use of social media? Does it make sense for you as a lawyer to be spending from 5 minutes to 2 hours a day on your phone and/or computer posting your lunch and sharing about your practice?

Maybe.

Here's the reality for most of us: the majority of our followers are already converts and know what we do. The friends from college, and our family don't need to know that you were in court today and "kicked the other guy's butt!" as a reminder to them that you're a Personal Injury lawyer. The people that don't know you that well,will likely never refer a client to you, because they have someone in their life who is closer emotionally that does the type of law you do.

So relax on the social media. Use it for what it's good for: keeping up to date with those closest to you, and don't worry about the distant 'friends and followers'. Maybe they'll send you some business, but not likely.

Facebook

This is the Big Dog in the Dog Park of Social Media and it's very tempting to spend a great deal of time and money here. Be very thoughtful about this because the Facebook controllers have tightly constricted the amount of exposure you can get without paying them.

Your basic posting on the wall about your huge court win, is probably going to be seen by about 10% of your friends. If it receives a lot of 'Likes' and the engagement with commenting is strong, they may boost, or more likely they will ask you to boost it, for a fee.... Again ,whose interest is that in? Not yours.

Promoted pages and postings are very expensive and don't reach as many people as we'd like. Yes we can pay more, and using their backend we can in theory do some amazing targeting, but as lawyers, you're probably not going to be a "BUY NOW" purchase. You're more likely to be a long term, educated choice and the display ads you pay for on Facebook are just not helping you find legal clients.

Twitter

Twitter is designed for short messages and links to webpages. Personally I think that this service is good as a newsreader to aggregate information on subjects you want to follow. As a means of advertising or promotion for attorneys - I don't see it. I've had a twitter account for years and I use it to search for articles of interest to me. I occasionally post about what is happening in my life, but mostly it's an outlet for cross-posting from my Instagram account.

Twitter is probably great for bars and nightclubs that want to push out messages to a known customer list about that night's entertainment or weekly bar special. I can't imagine anyone going on it looking for legal representation.

LinkedIN

This is the professional's place for real marketing and promotion. LinkedIN is the best of Facebook in a professional setting. This is where those posts about the latest new case law can be useful. This is where you can find affinity groups that will support your particular area of practice and if there's not one that is on point for you, build it! Odds are that if you are an expert on a subject, there's a need for a group on it.

LinkedIN will allow you to be a member of up to 50 groups with their paid models so you have the opportunity to really extend that reach into new markets because each group is unlimited in the number of members it can have. So while you may be limited in your professional connections, your group connections can be extended much further.

There is a built-in premium sales tool that is highly recommended for those who have a service or product that demands higher levels of targeting - Sales Navigator. Of course this comes at an additional cost, but if you want to do some very targeted networking, and drill down into exactly your perfect clients, whether individuals or companies, Sales Navigator is the key to identifying those targets.

Pinterest

The arts and crafts social media channel. This is where recipes, crochet and projects can be found that will keep you and those children busy on a rainy weekend. Each account comes with Boards and Pins so you can collect projects, recipes and information of value that you want to share with your community.

I used Pinterest for a while to build a recipe collection, and some projects of interest for topics of podcasts and blog entries. I lost interest in the channel quickly though and for marketing my practice, I don't think it was a good fit.

That said, if I was a construction defect law firm I may consider using it as a way to reach people who are most likely to have remodeled a kitchen or bath, and have contractor problems. If you represent plaintiffs in product liability cases, you may find an audience here with people sharing horror stories about appliances. For those who are disability attorneys, this site may be the place to find potential clients who are stuck at home recuperating and need better representation in their Worker's Compensation Cases or against the Social Security. If you do Veteran's Affairs type of work, reaching vets through the "Man Cave" or "Survival Skills" pins could be an avenue.

Generally though, I don't think this is where people will go looking for professional or legal services. It's more for domestic living than a business site.

CLIENT RELATIONS

Keeping up with clients is important if you want to maintain the referral mindset in them. There are two levels though of attention in my mind: 1)there's the base level of general contact, like newsletters, holiday cards etc.; and 2) the more valuable but time consuming and expensive is the personal touch. It's lunches, golfing, racquetball, attendance at clubs, sporting events, and gifting.

Newsletters

The dreaded monthly newsletter is a pain the rear for most small to mid-sized firms that lack a dedicated marketing person. It takes a real effort to put together a quality newsletter that has interesting and engaging content, an appealing design and then to either print and mail hard copies or coordinate the email system that does the mass distribution.

That's why there are services out there that will "white label" content for you. That means they have a stock newsletter they put out each month based on your area of specialty, and then just drop in your logos and branding. I'm not a big fan of that, because I think the clients see right through it as a nondescript piece of content that lacks your personal style and the reasons why they like you in the first place. It makes sense, since the writing for a stock newsletter is going to be as bland and personality-less as possible so that it can apply to the widest possible number of attorneys or firms.

Your personality is crucial to keeping the connection with your clients. They know who you are, and they want to hear and see from you that same style and uniqueness. Imagine Gerry Spence sending out a boring newsletter that discussed the latest interpretation of Miranda in stark, clinical legalese - it wouldn't work. It would be spotted as a fake in no time. Now that same topic with Gerry's signature style and touches of his sardonic humor and a good dose of his whoop-ass and now you have something people want to read.

The same goes for you. Don't be afraid to use your personality and to push it. That's why your clients are your clients.

Lunches and Golfing, etc.

"Never eat alone." It's something I strive for, and frankly I succeed most days. The reason why you should always have a lunch date is that breaking bread is a human connection that binds us closer. It's those languid conversations over some pasta, or the sheer fun of Korean BBQ that brings people together and keeps you top of mind, so when they are asked if they know a good attorney who does... you come to mind.

I'm not a golf guy. But I know the reason for golf is the three hours of uninterrupted time you get to have with someone as you play 18 holes. When else are you going to have that amount of one on one contact with a CEO or Vice President of HR? never.

My partner is a fisherman, so he does the fishing thing with people. Half-days on his boat, preferably far enough out that the cellphones wont work, and he can just chat with people.

Ask yourself what it is that you enjoy, and then find a way to incorporate that into your marketing outreach program. For me, it's breakfasts, lunches and dinners. For you it could be hunting, birding, or photography. Find a way to make a connection with your top clients and add it into your routine. You'll be amazed at the results.

Holiday Cards

The traditional holiday card is an old standby. I've had them specially printed, and I've gone to the stationery store and bought 500 in different packs. The only thing that truly matters is this: make sure the envelopes are hand addressed, and the cards are hand signed. Anything less just screams that we're phoning this in as a "must do" because our marketing team is trying to justify their salaries. It's expensive, time-consuming and so worth it.

Think about your own experience. In today's age of email and mass-market mass-produced "customized" messaging, don't you notice when someone has taken the time to send you a handwritten Thank You note? I know I do, because they are so very rare. I immediately raise my estimation and love for someone when they have taken 3 minutes to write me a note. Same goes for your holiday cards.

Gifts

Attorney gifting is generally poorly done. To learn how and why you should be gifting I recommend you read the book **Giftology** by John Ruhlin. He's a corporate gifting specialist and his company is the gold standard for making an impression. Ruhlin shared that in November his company stops sending out gifts to their clients. His reasoning is pure genius - any gift you send is a) probably going to be lost in a sea of others, and b) has a tinge of "obligation" to it because "it's the season!"

His company starts sending out gifts in February for unexpected reasons and at non-traditional times so that the impact of the gift is maximized.

Frankly it makes a great deal of sense to me, and I've transformed my gifting philosophy as a result of this teaching.

PROMOTIONAL ITEMS

The Swag we buy and give away, so that someone else can throw it away. Yup, I said it. Honestly how many "swag bags" are sitting in your office that will eventually be thrown out? The host had a great idea and the best of intentions in creating their swag for you, and that stainless steel water bottle with their logo isn't really a gift to you so much as it's a way for them to continue marketing and advertising in your office. Eventually you know you're going to throw it out, or give it away. Either way, was that money well spent by the giver? Probably not.

Business Cards

Some things are really important, like business cards. I still believe in them and I think you should have either a very simple and clear card, or one that really stands out. I have both. My original lawyer card has very traditional serif fonts, gold foil and is set up as a vertical card.

The latest card I designed and use for the MensFamilyLaw.com website is a four panel card that has my picture on it, the addresses for all my podcasts, videos and an entire panel that can be used to take notes.

I've spent hundreds of dollars on cards, and they make an impression upon the receiver. My four panel MensFamilyLaw card always gets noticed by the clerks because it is so big and clear. Prospects all notice and comment on it because it gives them so much information about what I do and how I can help them.

What do your cards say about you? Are they boring standard lawyer cards? Review them and for a few hundred dollars get something that helps you stand out.

Websites

Websites are the electronic brochure to your business. Most of them suck. They're boring repetitive and look like all the other law firms with the stereotypical ME ME ME focus on why the lawyers are the bestest, smartest, most aggressive, winningest lawyers and you should hire ME ME ME.

Ick.

The client who has questions, concerns and is looking for information needs a website that hits their emotional hot buttons, answers their crucial questions and provides value, value, value to them.

MensFamilyLaw.com

The MensFamilyLaw.com website is designed to give

men the answers they need and want in whatever form they want to learn it in. I have a Free "Before You Leave" download guide, there are books for them to buy and download right then so they can get the immediate answers a man in emotional crisis wants. I have podcast episodes for them to listen to. There are blog entries for those guys who like to read, and I have a whole video series for clients that want to watch short videos that are designed to address the most common questions and concerns.

By the time a man has gone through my website, they're either ready to hire us, or they hate us and will go somewhere else - either way, I'm good. I know I have a fan or a hater. One is going to work well with me, and one would be a disaster for both of us, so better he finds out early and moves on.

This is my main website and is built on the Wordpress platform which is the most robust and durable platform that I know of. I like it because there are many people who specialize in servicing it, and I'm not beholden to any one particular webmaster.

FamilyLawSeminars.com

We have a seminar website that is a very simple site, designed on the Weebly platform, so that I can make edits from my phone. I can literally be sitting in an airport lounge and redesign a page or the entire website over a cup of coffee and a bagel. I like having this level of control, and it works because it's a highly focused site that answers the need of the visitor. For the $150 a year it costs me to have the Weebly platform, it's well worth it.

InternationalChildCustody.com

We have a sub-sub-specialty in international child custody cases. They are a rarity, but I built a website for them, also on the Wordpress platform. Someone who is having an international issue, likely will search for the terms International, Child Custody, and by having the website that incorporates all those keywords, we rank high Google for these case inquiries.

InterstateChildCustody.com

Similarly we have a sub-sub-specialty in interstate child custody and child support cases. They are far more common, so I built a website for them, also on the Wordpress platform. Someone who is having an interstate issue, may search for the terms Interstate, Child Custody, or Child Support and by having the website that incorporates all those keywords, we rank high Google for these case inquiries.

DomesticAbuseDefense.com

The sad reality is that in today's family law courts, the Domestic Violence Restraining Order has become almost a Standard Operating Procedure for someone who wants to get an advantage in court over their soon-to-be ex and the children. Because we primarily represent men, we are more often on the defense side, so

I decided to build out a website for these issue as well.

Brochures

The traditional print brochure is not dead, just 'mostly dead' (that's a Princess Bride reference for those of us who have reached a certain age!). Primarily we use them when I attend an event like the Handel on the Law- Law Day or some other mixer.

We have the four color, glossy, offset printed kind of brochure. If you are going to be doing a lot of mass market promotions like mixers, I recommend you have a professionally designed and printed brochure. It's worth the money, if your services are a high enough ticket.

Footballs

The MensFamilyLaw logo was designed to be evocative of the NFL. Its color scheme is primary blue and red, it has a shield that will evoke the connection. So when I was looking for a promotional item to give away I found squeezee balls in the shape of a football, and that was a perfect promo item for us. I've given away an untold amount over the years, and people keep them because they are fun and they tie in with the overall mission of our marketing.

Condoms

So you had to know I was going to do this one. It's just too delicious, as a family law attorney, especially one that focuses on men, condoms are a natural promotional item - yet, I had a battle on my hands with my partner. He's more conservative than I am, and he felt they would be too risqué, too unseemly and crass. So in the interests of business harmony, I held off. But I never gave up (kind of a personal trait of mine!) I knew I wanted them, and I knew that they would work.

So a few years back I was attending the inaugural Podcast Movement conference. It's an event designed to serve podcasters, a group that skews HEAVILY to the men. Here was my chance. It's perfect I thought, it's a unique cultural group, it'll be out of state since the conference is in Dallas, and I'll only get a few hundred made.

The partner relented and let me try this. Huge success! I had taken them and put them around the convention, in the planters in the men's rooms I'd hand them out to guys after I introduced myself. I was known throughout the convention as the 'condom guy' - it doesn't get better than that!

Pens

Pens, pens, everyone wants pens. Boring, boring, boring. Yes we've done them. Yes they're cheap as a giveaway, I just question they're effectiveness. I have a box full of pens that I have collected over the years from other businesses and frankly I never look to them when I'm looking for a service provider.

I stopped having them made because I think that it's a waste of money and effort. I'd rather have something memorable, like condoms. And that would be my advice to you, find something that is different and will set you apart. The pens are simply not going to do it.

Books

Outside of your professional designation, "Author" is likely the most powerful descriptor you will have in developing credibility with your prospects. It's an instant marker that you are expert, and you have staked out a territory to declare your expertise.

In 2000, when I started writing books, the world of self-publishing looked vastly different. To print your own books meant minimum print runs, high expense with the layout, the printing and storage and shipping of books. It was much more of commitment if you wanted to do it.

My first attempt at self-publishing is a good story...

Family Law Handbook

I've always loved writing, so it was obvious to me that as a newly minted lawyer what would be a good marketing tool would be a book on Family Law. I compiled several of the articles I had written for the Santa Monica Daily Press and put them into a Microsoft Word document and shipped it off to Kinko's for printing.

Yes, my first book was 8 1/2 by 11 pages, with a tape binding. No it was not pretty. Horrifically ugly is a better description - but it was my first book.

Entrepreneur's Handbook

My second book was a larger project. I worked my way through law school doing small business turn-arounds (fixing companies that were in trouble) so I had a lot of content that I wanted to share with the world. This time, my book was going to have GRAPHICS! Well the best graphics that I could find in my Word program. Highly pixelated, cartoony, graphics that I shudder at today.

BUT. I was now an author with bookS! PLURAL! Ugly, oversized, poorly made, books, but there were two of them.

Estate Planning Handbook

My third effort was still in the large format, but I lost the graphics, kept the tape binding…These books were relatively inexpensive to produce at Kinko's and made a good take-away piece for those events where we had rented a booth and were talking to the public. Over the years, those ugly books have led to new clients so they have definitely paid for themselves.

A Man's Guide series

Self-publishing took a giant leap forward in the 2000's with this new concept of Print On Demand. Computers and printers had advanced to the point where it was now economically feasible to print a book, one at at time. (Gutenberg would be astounded I'm sure at what we can do today!)

The age of the laptop and computer design had ushered in a new ability of anyone to design and layout a book, a book cover and upload it a server that would then print it and thanks to FedEx, ship it overnight anywhere in the world.

I know my audience - men. I know they are not going to read a giant treatise on the intricacies of family law strategy. So I wrote a series of books designed with their needs and wants in mind:

A Man's Guide to Divorce Strategy

A Man's Guide to Child Custody, and

A Man's Guide to Domestic Violence.

I designed the covers with strong colors and images that would convey the subject matter. The books themselves would be written in concise language, the biggest book is just over 110 pages, in large print, with tall line spacing to make it easy to read and take notes. I figured most men would be reading them while they were in a state of emotional crisis, having just been served with a Summons and Petition or a Domestic Violence Restraining Order and their normally low attention span would be even more impacted due to the stress of the new situation.

If I were to write a book for a female audience I would do the exact opposite. I would write a book that has every possible situation and tactic covered. I would include loads of additional information, examples of declarations and motions, and make the book about 400 pages. It's the difference in attitude, between a female client and a male client. He wants the situation "fixed", she knows what result she wants, because she's done the research.

The reason I write all this is that, like Harold Hill in the musical, The Music Man, "You Gotta Know Your Territory." Write for your audience. Don't try and give them what they wont read, it just frustrates you and annoys them.

What About Wally

My sixth book was a collaboration with a former client who came to me and said "I want to do a book about pets in divorce and how we share the dog." My immediate emotional reaction was that's stupid, but what came out of my mouth, as the reality dawned on me, was, "That's a GENIUS idea!"

I had done his divorce and they shared their dog. Years earlier, the first divorce I ever mediated, the dog was a (Pardon the phrasing) bone of contention. In my own breakup, we negotiated the terms of dog-sharing. So even though my first emotion was "this is stupid" in milliseconds I realized that it is actually a rather common issue.

So we wrote a book about it called What About Wally? Co-Parenting A Pet With An Ex. The first half of the book is a memoir of my story with my former boyfriend, and how we share our dog. The second half is a parenting plan that I reworked from our standard Child

Custody Parenting Plans. We hired a book designer for the interior and a cover designer for the front image of a golden lab with two leashes coming off it, one pink and one blue.

The book story went viral and we were featured in papers and magazines all across the globe. Yes I can honestly say I have been on the front of the Kuwait Times!

To this day I receive phone calls and emails from people who find the book and want me to be either an expert consultant on their reality that's "in development" or to help them with their personal custody battles. I think we were a bit ahead of the curve, and it was only in 2018/2019 that the courts in California caught up to the need for pet custody to be decided by family courts.

Documentary Films

Living in Los Angeles, there's no way to avoid the entertainment industry - like water, it will find its way in. For me, that has been on both sides of the camera.

Govt vs. Green

One of my clients decided to build his own electric car. From scratch. He rented an old garage and started building, but he had a neighbor who was just a beast. And somehow the DMV, the Santa Monica Fire Department and the Santa Monica Police department were alerted to an illegal car manufacturer. This resulted in "raid" one day on his shop/garage. It was a giant waste of government money, time and effort that went nowhere. So of course a movie must be made about it.

I was his lawyer, and that means I'm interviewed which means that I'm now an expert on the extremely niche field of home-grown car manufacturing. (It's not a growth industry by the way!)

It was fun, and I do have an IMDB (Internet Movie Database) entry as a result of it.

What About the Men? - Crowdfunding Campaigns

After a decade of representing men in court defending various allegations against them that were lodged under the Domestic Violence Prevention Act, I realized that there was a real problem. Men don't see themselves as targets of domestic abuse (I try not to use the "V" word - victim - because it's too polarizing for men) and society (or at least most judges and Petitioner's counsel) see them as aggressors.

But any honest expert in the domestic violence industry will tell you it's a highly complex issue that has many nuances. So I started to produce a documentary about the male side of the equation when they were attacked.

Funding a documentary is not an easy task, but this is the age of the internet and we have GoFundMe, IndieGoGo and a host of other solutions to crowdfund projects and artistic endeavors.

I knew I needed about $5,000, so I started to fundraise

on IndieGoGo and ran it for two weeks, which gave me a great reason to promote myself and my topic on Facebook and LinkedIN and Twitter. The exposure was great and I received a tremendous response to the campaign and we made our goal.

Would I do it again? Only with a team of social media experts behind me. The truth is that the exposure is great, but it's a LOT of work. Posting 4-8 times a day on social media, and creating content that continues to be engaging is exhausting. If I were ever to attempt it again I would spend an additional month planning the launch and the execution, maybe two months.

But I don't regret the experience and it helped get my name out there as an expert on domestic violence and it opened doors for me with public officials that I wanted to reach.

CONCLUSION

Writing this book has been a fun trip down memory lane with all the various things that I have done to bring in new clients. I've remembered things that I forgot about, and people that slipped from memory. As you can see I've tried just about everything, and many of them I've tried in different ways to see if it worked better. Sometimes a marketing tactic didn't work well at first (my first books!) but as I refined and polished it, we had better results.

Lessons Learned

If I had to share ONE lesson that I have learned from all of this, it is that you have to remember it's all a Slot Machine, not a Gumball Machine.

But there are other lessons I want to reinforce with you:

Take Chances - almost no one will remember those

giant fails that you've tried in a month. And if they do remember there's a good lesson in that - it was memorable!

Try Again - No one ever learned to walk in a day. Yet everyone knows how. Your first efforts will be shaky, wonky, and yes you'll be embarrassed by them in a year - that's okay! Be embarrassed. Your ugliest start is better than the perfect that never gets shared.

People Need You - Truly. What you do is important and if you do not let them know how you can help them, you're just wasting your talents, skills and abilities. How many people are you not helping but could if you overcame your shyness and insecurity?

Be the good, be of service, and know that it will come back to you, just probably not from where you think, I can almost guarantee that. In my experience the more I give away, the more I receive, and from usually the unlikeliest of sources.

So with that in mind, I share this with you…

HOW CAN I HELP YOU ?

I'm like a modern day, male version of Dolly Levi from the play Hello Dolly! I like to go around and encourage young things to grow. If I can help you, let's find a way to work together.

2 Hour consultation

Generally it takes about two hours for the real relationship potential to reveal itself. I have to know enough about you, and you need to know how I operate to begin to see the synergies and possibilities. If this sounds like something you'd like to explore, I offer a two hour coaching session so that we can determine what your goals are, and how we can work together.

Marketing Plan

If you know you need a marketing plan, and want help with developing one that will fit your particular area of speciality I'm happy to set up a time to get started on building your firm and practice to best suit your life goals.

Monthly Mastermind

I also run monthly Mastermind groups which are based on the Napoleon Hill model of people coming together weekly or monthly, for a common purpose. Usually it is to discuss a specific business topic. Traditionally there are a variety of professionals in the group, (Therapist, Accountant, Lawyer, etc) so it becomes a great way to get to know people and create referral sources.

I add in a structure that brings focus to each meeting and concentrates on individual needs with a "hot seat" that rotates each week for members to have a 360 review of their business by the other members. Some of my Masterminds are solely for lawyers, because we need to speak freely about client issues, and some are with a general business group.

Find Your Legal Exit Strategy

Lastly, if you're completely burned out, and need to leave your practice, but have obligations like a family, a mortgage, partners, etc, you need an exit strategy. We can work together to find your true passions, and turn that into a business that will allow you to leave the high stress, unsatisfying career you're in.

You have more options than you think you have. The problem is you cannot see them, because of the Fog of War. When you're in the middle of a war, it's very difficult to see the path to victory. That's why you need an outside perspective that has experience and vision. Together we can create a life that will reward you and bring happiness to you and your family.

Don't forget that as a Thank You, you have a month of free email coaching with me!

I hope you've found this book to be useful and I look forward to meeting you and working with you!

Best Wishes for your Happiness and Success!

David T. Pisarra, Esq.

P.S. Drop me an email to get started on your month of free coaching, or if you have questions, comments or just want to say HI!

david@GlobalBusinessCoaching.com

PROFESSIONAL SPEAKING ENGAGEMENTS

If your law firm or organization needs a keynote or breakout speaker for an upcoming leadership retreat, conference of annual meeting, David Pisarra is available as professional speaker on the subjects of:

- **Leadership for Lawyers**

- **Podcasting for Professionals**

- **Legal Marketing**

He is a member of the National Speakers Association and has spoken in SIX countries on the topic of Podcasting for Professionals.

David's speaking website is www.DavidPisarra.com where there are testimonials and examples of his speaking ability and style.

TO CONTACT DAVID TO SPEAK:

David Pisarra, Esq.

310-664-9969

David@GlobalBusinessCoaching.com